A JOURNEY OF QUOTES

Fact

The world has become more unpredictable.

Adam Ralstein a first time Author based in bulawayo, Zimbabwe. A visionary man who saw a need to write a book on quotes to help encourage, give hope and lead people to a better way of life.

A journey of quotes

Life is a journey full of choices. Where we end up can be summed up by the decisions we make along the way.

A quote a day keeps us happy along the way.

You can chat with Adam on

Twitter @CoachAdam5

Facebook Adam Ralstein

LinkedIn Adam Ralstein

Instagram Adam Ralstein

Email: ralsteinadam@gmail.com

A JOURNEY OF QUOTES

by

Adam Ralstein

AELIN PUBLISHERS
INDIA

AELIN PUBLISHERS
India

Published by Aelin Publishers India

This is a work of fiction. Names, characters, places, businesses, and incidents are products of the author's imagination or used in a fictitious manner. Any resemblance to any actual person, living or dead, events or locales is entirely coincidental.

ISBN 978-81-953782-0-3

www.aelinpublishers.com
Email: aelinpublishers@gmail.com
Instagram/Twitter: aelinpublishers

When the individual is not ready, opportunity moves on.

The journey's short, so make it worthwhile.

You are the lords prized possession even in the storm.

Your paycheck is normally a reflection of your knowledge acquired.

Manage people in a manner that brings out the best of them.

The perfect sacrifice that sets us free.

The spirit of the lord is moving and those called are been awakened to a life in christ.

It's possible that our walk or rather way of life could be holding back our blessings.

One should always check what energy you bring to the table. Do you leave people drained or energized? Do the words you speak uplift or destroy the listener?

Strive by all means not to be the source of someone's pain, least you be held accountable by he who sees all.

We are shaped by our surroundings and oftentimes we compromise to suit the standards of this time. As believers we are called to stand out, a light in this dark world.

You can be exceptionally good at something and yet bad at teaching what you good at.

One cannot dance in the dark and yet expect to be blessed in the light.

Be the person God intended you to be.

Let your start up stage be an inspiration to where you want to end up.

Faith by divine connection. A deeper connection with the almighty is the foundation faith is build on.

Let yourself open before Christ and let him build a better version of you.

It's your duty not to serve outdated thinking and methods of doing things.

The enemy may have marked you for a period, but the lord has ear marked you for greatness.

The mind and body can struggle with something for years upon years. Yet a small nudge from the holy spirit will set the motion to overcome all hindrances.

Your dependence on Christ is your strength.

Life is like a photo, sometimes you got to be the background.

Change can only take place when the mind and soul are in sync.

Life is a journey and the choices we make determines the view.

We would have a lot more people turning to Christ, if we the believers were more loving and less judgmental.

People don't always come straight out to destroy your dreams. They come looking innocent to plant a seed of doubt.

The body and mind are a reflection of what you feed them.

In every situation in life, someone makes money.

Your mercy stretches further than the mind can comprehend.

The system is designed to create workers at the expense of entrepreneurs.

Movement based on faith. This act of doing something, knowing Christ will back the action.

We are only here for a short time. Live your dream and don't feel bad about it.

Nothing dramatic has to happen to you to change your way of life. Just make a choice to walk in a way pleasing to God.

I believe in our lifetime, we are to change at least one person's life in a positive manner.

God's ways also apply to the financial side of life. Make all your dealings with money clean.

You don't need to keep looking around for reasons to quit something that's not good for you. Just quit.

You are shaped by your habits.

Take control of the weekend, it is where the devil's hand rests heavy.

In times of Great trouble, Animals turn to humans for help. In times of trouble, humans turn to God for help. It's the circle of life.

There's no form of sugar coating that can make something the lord has termed wrong to be right.

How long can we hold on to thorns and not bleed? Some situations just need you to remove yourself.

How long can we hold on to thorns and not bleed? We are our biggest enemies by holding on to things that actually harm us.

Forgiveness plays a vital role on how a soul stands in christ.

We can come to know christ through the reading of his word. By not reading, we remove a great amount of understanding who he is.

It's an honor to do that which is right in the lord's eyes.

We are just but a breath, may your days be filled with love, joy, peace, and happiness.

Guilt with no change of action is feather light.

Part of our daily walk is owning up to our sins.

Your speech at any time reflects the state of mind and condition of the heart. Pay attention.

You are not a voice piece for people's lives.

This world has raised us up to persecute those who have a right standing with the lord. Yet these are the people we must cherish on our journey home.

Some of the vessels the lord has chosen to deliver his message are unpolished. Your life changing message today could come from an unexpected source.

Where warnings have been given, we have nothing to hold on to once caught up.

Be careful what you water, weeds also grow.

What you nurture, grows.

The quality of your work is a part of your success story.

You don't have to do what your parents did to be deemed a success.

We only here for a season, let's make it rain.

Open your mind to learning other ways of achieving success.

The blessings of the lord go further than the mind can comprehend.

Keeping the lord's ways becomes easier when we find it a delight to spend time in his presence.

We often pray for the finished product, of which the lord provides us with the means to achieve this. Part of life's journey is building on what the lord has provided.

The mind is good in creating comforting excuses.

Potential is as good as an unearthed Diamond.

Righteousness based on love. The love for christ, that keeps you following his ways.

Your boat is sinking because the load you carrying is too heavy. This is the same with you, take the time to analyze the dead weight you carrying around. It serves no purpose, offload your boat.

A relationship with the lord is talking to him daily, It involves making decisions based on his word and laying all before him, both good and bad.

In all our troubles and afflictions, God remains God.

We have a duty to draw closer to christ. In his presence we have life.

If half of marital problems are finances, then a man must only commit when he is financially strong.

No one understands a call for help better than our Lord and savior Jesus Christ.

A large number of humanity will always remain weak. Mainly because they are limited by their thoughts.

Nothing consumes a man more, than having a heart filled with hatred.

The lords blessings fall heavy on the straight and narrow road.

Progression involves channeling your energy in the right direction. One should always monitor both time and effort as in the long run both have a effect on our livelihood.

There's a thin line between forgiving and forgetting. He who forgives, must also master the art of forgetting the grievance.

All teachers of the Gaspel, must have a foundation of love for the word of God to move forward.

Situations will change from time to time but we must never allow them to affect our belief system.

Eating fatty foods may be unhealthy, but so is a toxic mouth. Food can be digested, words last a lifetime.

One should always be weary of people who try to make you feel guilty or bad about someone's success.

The words you speak out, determine your path. Victory is always close, for those who are guided by a positive tongue.

The words you speak out determine your footsteps. The steps of the victories are guided by a positive tongue.

A starving man will appreciate the gospel more if it comes with groceries. If you have the means to meet a direct need and spread the gospel, then do so. All glory be to God.

Long before depression settles in, the mind begins to create a pattern of unhappiness. If unchecked, a solid foundation is formed and every thought is subject to sadness.

If there's one thing each soul should be weary of, is never be responsible for someone's tears.

The mind is always ready to be pushed to the next level. The key is taking the first step.

A greater season of prayer is needed in these times. The enemy whose time is short, is closing in quicker than ever seen before.

One day everything will just make sense and you will know your purpose. When that day comes, don't fight the holy spirit but embrace the power.

Those coming out of a dark place need to be nurtured as they adjust to the light. Let the love of God lead the way.

A lot of our hindrances are self-inflicted. One should take the time to analyse our shortfalls and the causes. Thus, making the necessary changes.

The words you speak out, determine your path. The footsteps of the positive, often end in victory.

Life is a journey in which we must strive to involve Christ every step of the way.

Sin comes dressed with everything our physical side is attracted to. Sin looks appealing on the outside and yet hides a destructive force within.

Each day provides the opportunity to walk in our lord's ways and be a light unto others.

One must understand, not everyone can handle power or a position of authority.

Exposure opens us to a world of opportunities. Try something new and reap the benefits.

One of the devil objectives is to make you disregard the power of prayer.

Those under the lord's wings, will experience success they can handle. Anything more, is open ground for the evil one to join.

Some of the people you show mercy, the lord has delivered them to be conquered.

We are fast moving to a stage, where believers now measure their level of righteousness against other people. Christ will always be the mark we look up to.

When small things make us happy, we have less sad days. He who appreciates the shoes he wears, won't dwell too much on the car he doesn't have.

When you place God where he needs to be in your life, only then can he place you, where you need to be.

Life would be so much simply, if we just stuck to doing what is right. We complicate our existence, by choosing to do what we know is wrong.

The Lord can be either your friend or your enemy, just depends which side of the fence you are.

The wisdom of the poor is rarely celebrated. Their voices go unheard in a world hooked on titles.

Tell me more about Christ and his journey on earth and less about your church and why I should join you.

Lights shine best in the dark. A lot of the times, you are the Lord's light in a dark place.

The only stamp of approval I seek is the one from Christ.

The understanding of God's word is a journey at times we read the map and still choose to take the wrong direction. Other times we stick to the coordinates and a relationship is built thus guiding us home safely.

It's the weekends spent at home relaxed that really count. No need to spread ourselves thin to feel alive.

Decisions made for Christ are as sure as his second coming.

Don't loose hope. There is a day written with your name in which the Lord will bring the biggest smile your face ever experienced.

There is an unseen law that operates in the beginning of most relationships. One will begin to like the other a bit more and show more affection, this in turn normally leads to the other person pulling away. If treating someone with more love, causes them to pull away and neglecting someone causes them to be drawn closer, is the system flawed? By no means, the above message applies to relationships dominated by the flesh. Where the spirit operates, there is clarity and understanding.

Be careful of those loud and quite voices, telling you your vision not worth the effort. Some come in the form of family and friends.

If necessary, the Lord will strategically place and send some formidable enemies, to change your route and save you from the road you've chosen.

The greater enemy we face is not the devil himself but the inner being that chooses to operate outside the boundaries of God's word.

How deep do words uttered in anger go? That they can cause another soul, years down line to breakdown when they remember them. Take time to reason before you speak against another soul.

There is something special about waking up at 5AM and letting those knees touch the ground. The quietness of the morning allows the spirit to connect with the father at a higher level.

The night holds many secrets only the true light will expose.

If 10 people with your exact character traits were put in one room, would you greet each other, would you become friends? A key to understanding who we are, is we must imagine a world with only people like us, would they be peace, would love easily flow...Growth begins when you can view yourself as is and make the necessary changes.

Some people are so convinced over the power they believe they have over you. Learn to surprise them such power only belongs to God who is immortal.

One of the greatest gifts of love the Lord has given his creation is the freedom of choice. Yet that freedom can elevate some and cause some to be locked up in chains of despair. Nevertheless, God is love.

If only you knew how valuable you are in God's eyes, you wouldn't be content with some of the things you settle for.

Character and strength come from different seasons we face in life, as each season comes with its own lessons.

If trials and tribulations cause our knees to hit the floor and seek Christ more, then they will always be there.

Everyone desires to be happy, deserves to be loved and have a sense of meaningful existence. Most believe that happiness can be found in the tangible things we aquire while we walk this dusty Earth. A selected few realise happiness is the peace of mind you have by being comfortable in your surroundings.

Very few people rejoice when you find a partner as compared to when a relationship ends within this phrase is the hidden agenda of man's heart and what excites him.

The Devil's first priority is to eliminate game changers. Isolate the Shepherd and scatter the sheep.

The greatest battle each believer will have to conquer, is doing what is right in the Lord's eyes, over what we feel is right.

I believe its God's will to bless his children when they are ready. Many of us pray for blessings we are not ready to receive. Blessings will always be delayed until the receiver is ready.

You may have fallen down to the ground, but remember that's where great trees start. You are in a perfect place to start all over again, relying on God's power.

The Devil and his fallen angels have only set one goal and that is to stop as many as they can from Eternal life under the father.

Not everyone is earmarked to reach great heights or to be highly successful, but each believer is responsible for making Christ known to those within the sphere of influence.

Take time out of each day to check up on people, encourage them and show them that you care. A lot of smiles you see out there, hide deep pains that only acts of love can release under the guidance of the holy spirit.

Head to Toe prayer

Heavenly father guide my mind so as to set it on things of above.

Let it be focused on eternal things and not the temporary things this world has to offer.

May I always place you within the center of my heart influencing all my acts of love.

Lead my feet to pursue righteousness all the days of my life.

Every man must come to a end of self, for God to start a great work in him. It is only when we are fully dependent on the Lord, can we experience great victories.

Each believer has the responsibility to show the love of Christ, to those they come into contact with.

The key to any successful relationship, is to understand you are dating someone whose not you. You may have similar beliefs or core values, but still differ in a number of ways. Embrace the uniqueness.

God has chosen people set aside to achieve his will and nothing that comes their way will stop them from achieving it.

A church which does not show love to its visitors will not have new members. Part of the reason visitors become members is the love shown by the congregation. It's as simple as that. Teach the congregation to be loving and welcoming to the visitors.

A church system that does not incorporate love, will have its sphere of influence cut, regardless of the message of truth it gives out.

Having a judgemental spirit will open your eyes to the sins of others and yet close them to your very own sins.

We sometimes choose to walk through fire, then blame God when we get burnt.

The best person you can ever be is becoming the person God intended you to be.

1+1=2. We all know this because we've been taught this. Now to him who has been taught 1+1=3, in his eyes there is no other way. The above is a clear example of how false doctrine affects a believer. It will have you believing and defending is a lie.

It takes a strong mind to go against the flow of the world. By spending more time with Christ, we begin to realise, what the world offers is temporary.

The Devil and his fallen angels were kicked out of heaven because they failed to keep the laws in heaven. Sin is the transgression of the law. Had no law existed in heaven, the Devil and his fallen angels would not be held accountable for their sins.

Each and everyone alive today is blessed with a spiritual gift or gifts from the holyspirit. Yet the way we use our gifts are limited if we don't allow love to accompany them. One who is blessed with the gift of healing, will only heal a few if he lacks love. One who is blessed with the gift of teaching, will only teach a few if his message lacks love.

One thing we must all come to understand, is not every open door is for you. The devil opens doors too, with one goal of leading you away from Christ.

Jesus when tempted by the Devil after spending 40 days and 40 nights in the wilderness fasting, simply defended himself by using the word of God. Too many of us are falling today because we stand firm on human reasoning.

During creation a woman was the only living soul created from what was already created. God could have also simply formed the woman from the dust, but he saw it fitting that one of man's ribs be removed to form a woman.

Only through the power of the holy spirit, can we learn to forgive whole heartedly. At some stage in life, everyone will encounter someone they find hard to forgive. It is at this time we should seek Christ through his spirit, who is able to guide us into total forgiveness.

Any one can become addicted to something but not anyone can free themselves once addicted. It's only by the power of God that strongholds, fortified walls and chains are broken.

As a child of God, you will meet many battles if your only desire to be a Christian is to be saved. As Christians we are to be a example of love, by leading others to Christ.

Your enemy or enemies may have their eyes on you but so does God. We can take refuge with the fact that nothing happens to us, unless ordained by God.

Some people may thing it's over for you, unbeknown to them, God has just started a good work in you. Stay strong, focused and happy in Christ.

Give time to reading the word of God, as this is where the lord opens himself to you and directs your path.

Deep down most individuals know what they need to do, to get back on the straight and narrow road. This can only happen if your desire to get back, exceed your desire to stay routed on a road with no rewards.

Only the peace God offers, can make you feel alright, when things are still and nothing is going your way.

Each person will give an account of themselves on judgement day. We tend to focus too much on other people's sins and shortcomings as if it would help aid us during the passing of our judgement.

1. Not everyone will get married.

2. Not everyone will have kids.

3. Not everyone will get to know Christ as lord and saviour.

4. Not everyone will understand their role in life.

5. Not everyone will be rich in this life.

6. Yet everyone is given life and a period of happiness.

You will be judged by many during your earthly lifespan. These judgements of cause, have no bearing on the final hot seat before God. Live a life that is pleasing to God, for his judgement opens or closes the door to eternity.

As believers we must be weary of putting ourselves on a pedestal, as if already saved. Too many believers have lost their earthly use, because of self exaltation. Jesus Christ came down to save all.

Only when you align your life with Gods will and abide in his ways, will you experience the fullness of life. They are countless blessings that come from standing firm on the word of God.

At times you are also someone's enemy because of your actions. We are accountable for the enemies we create by our own actions.

When you fast, you starve the flesh and feed the spiritual through prayer. Many forget that all breakthroughs begin in the spiritual realm.

At times the perfect peace is experienced after war.

God is a God of peace but can also operate within the boundaries of war. The Devil is the author of war but cannot operate within the boundaries of peace.

In church is where you will find people struggling with sin, broken people, unforgiving people and hypocrites. This is ok ofcause, as this is the right facility for all to find Jesus who is able to break all strongholds.

Many of our prayers are answered because we nurturing a seed of doubt. The Lord cannot move on doubt as this is opposite to how he operates.

If we dealt with matters of the heart based on facts, we would have less hurt people and less time wasted with the wrong person.

When the spirit leads the flesh, we have progress. When the flesh leads the spirit, we have setbacks and regrets. Who you allow to lead will have a huge bearing on who you become.

Ever wonder why at times the lord joins the battle late or rather allows the enemy to have his way with you for a while? The answer is simple, most believers go into the battle field dependent on their own strengths. The Devil quickly exhausts these strengths, which in turn causes the believer to seek a higher power. Seek the lord's intervention early.

Give a weak man money and he will often eat away from home. Give a weak woman a man whose gone broke and she will leave him. An increase or decrease in funds will show the strength of the foundation, a couple has built on.

The Bible says, before the end, the Gospel will be preached to the whole world. It also says, the Devil is filled with fury because he knows his time is short. Key points to understand.

1. *The Devil knows the Gospel will reach all, but his focus is to limit its effectiveness.*
2. *As much as the Devil's time is short, ours here on earth is shorter. Strive to spend it, within the boundaries of the Gospel.*
3. *Nothing here on Earth is worth losing Eternal life.*

We could all become better people by learning how to build up others, instead of tearing them down. A true reflection of character, is the ability to help lift up a burdened soul.

As we draw closer to the end of Earth's history, our savior is calling his people our of sin. He then places them strategically to be a influence unto many. The least expected people will begin to move strong on God's behalf.

Been kind is a act of love that every believer should show forth. The Bible says we will always have the poor amongst us. Take time to lesson other people's burdens, by giving freely what they lack. In doing so, your father in heaven is praised.

A enemy that shows you mercy when you in a vulnerable situation, was never really your enemy.

As believers we are encouraged to search the scriptures day and night as the bereans did. Church should never be the only time Gods word is opened.

Just as walking in the mud slows you down. So do some of the things you choose to align yourself with.

Gods way is blessed and those who walk within it are blessed too. You will find that most of life's mistakes are made when we step out of Gods way. To pursue our own agendas.

Most peoples biggest setbacks or regrets fall on the weekend. If you can conquer the weekend, you would have reached a high level of awakening.

Rejection loses its power when you understand that God has that special person for you, and will make things happen according to his will.

Some slept hungry today, but God saw it fit that you should eat today. Some woke up to the same menu, but God saw it fit, that you should have a choice this morning. Yet the one's with less, seek God more!!!

As believers we are encouraged to live a quiet and blameless life. This of course is not always easy in a fallen world. We represent Christ here on earth and our behaviour can either lead others to Christ or the opposite.

A common weakness with humanity, is people fall for the person who makes them feel less of themselves. We look closer, we realise both lack the understanding of love.

1. *If you love someone you will treat them right.*
2. *If you have self love, you won't settle for anything less than true love.*

A small example of how love, faith and obedience are connected to a believers walk in Christ.

1. *You cannot claim to love God, but are not obedient to his word.*
2. *You cannot have faith in a God you do not love.*
3. *You cannot be obedient to a God you have no faith in.*

Each believer will at least struggle with one of the three concepts in their lifetime. Ask the lord to strengthen you in your weak area.

A predators natural instinct to hunt is triggered by hunger and will to survive. Very few people are successful at what they do, because hunger is lacking.

We should pray for our leaders in high positions of authority. This is where the devils hand settles heavily upon. The enemy seeks to influence those who make decisions to go to war. Those who press buttons that kill thousands and those who sign in new laws outside Gods commands.

Trials come for two reasons.

1. *To test the foundation you have built on.*
2. *To show you only one foundation can withstand all trials.*

In case you were wondering, this foundation is Jesus Christ. Any other foundation will not stand the test of life itself.

All teachers have limits. It's the students responsibility to go further than what they have been taught.

www.ingramcontent.com/pod-product-compliance
Lightning Source LLC
Chambersburg PA
CBHW050025170726
48282CB00025B/555
* 9 7 8 8 1 9 5 3 7 8 2 0 3 *